BEWARE OF HYPOCRISY

Beware of Hypocrisy

Who Is Teaching Us What?

ROBERT WALIGURSKI

RESOURCE *Publications* · Eugene, Oregon

BEWARE OF HYPOCRISY
Who Is Teaching Us What?

Resource Publications
An Imprint of Wipf and Stock Publishers
199 W. 8th Ave., Suite 3
Eugene, OR 97401

www.wipfandstock.com

PAPERBACK ISBN: 978-1-5326-9173-7
HARDCOVER ISBN: 978-1-5326-9174-4
EBOOK ISBN: 978-1-5326-9175-1

Manufactured in the U.S.A.   JULY 25, 2019

Beware of the leaven of the Pharisees,
which is hypocrisy. For there is nothing
covered that will not be revealed,
nor hidden that will not be known.

LUKE 12:1-2

Contents

Introduction

For a time is coming when people will no longer listen to sound and wholesome teaching. They will follow their own desires and will look for teachers who will tell them whatever their itching ears want to hear.

2 TIMOTHY 4:3 (NLT)

MY PARENTS WERE RAISED in the Roman Catholic Church. They raised me in the Catholic Church as well. Neither my parents nor I ever completely read through the New Testament until we were older adults. Instead of studying the Scriptures for ourselves, we relied on the Catholic Church as our primary source for learning the teachings of Jesus. In hindsight, this was a huge mistake that I hope others who read *Beware of Hypocrisy* will avoid.

I wrote this book as a warning to those who learned all they know about Christianity from a church instead of through reading and studying the New Testament, especially the Gospels, themselves. Exclusively relying on one institution for such vital information can be dangerous, yet this seems to be a trend in our society. My hope is that this book will help you to understand why you should not fall into this trap.

After years of analyzing the teachings of Jesus as documented in both canonical manuscripts (i.e., ones accepted by the Church and included in the Bible) and non-canonical manuscripts (i.e., ones rejected from being included in the Bible), I am saddened by how much of what churches are teaching and doing appear to be contrary to these teachings of Jesus. After almost two thousand years of making assumptions and inventing doctrines, churches have subtly changed, over time, the teachings of Jesus into something different from what is presented in the Scriptures.

Despite the problems that will be discussed in this book, I have no desire to see the churches closed down, since they do provide vital services to humankind. They offer a mechanism where the community of faithful can gather to worship, pray, discuss Scripture, share Communion, support one another, and assist the needy. Furthermore, it is one of the best ways of introducing people to Christianity. However, I hope to see positive changes come about in the established churches and new churches coming into existence that better follow the teachings of Jesus as presented in the New Testament.

A Protestant pastor once told me that a large portion of his time is spent meeting with people seeking his consent to do something the Scriptures plainly say is a sin. Usually they think that their circumstances are unique or dire enough to warrant an exemption. They think if a church official can be convinced that their sin is justified, then God will think so also, thus soothing their conscience.

In a similar way throughout history, a constant pressure has been put upon churches, especially by emperors, kings, and other prominent individuals, to permit various sins. Once a church permits a sin for one individual, the sin usually becomes a part of that church's doctrine, permitting others to commit the sin seemingly guilt free.

Over the centuries, various denominations have declared different doctrinal stands regarding what is a sin and what is not. This is why so many different churches declare such wildly varied and oftentimes opposing doctrines. For example, some churches celebrate homosexual marriages, while others teach homosexuality is a mortal sin.

Modern churches have such diverse doctrines that people can now shop around for a church with teachings and doctrines that are copacetic with their chosen lifestyle. Because the Bible does not give specifics on every issue, people oftentimes demand the churches provide definite, unambiguous doctrine on all important issues so they can live their lives without questioning whether or not something they are doing, or not doing, is a sin. Churches need congregants for their survival; therefore, many have evolved to accommodate the desires of the masses.

My analysis approach throughout this book will be to first state the teachings of Jesus regarding a given topic, as presented in the Bible, and then contrast it with what churches teach and do regarding the subject. It is not my intent to present the churches' rationalizations/justifications for what they have done, assumed, or taught. Numerous publications are available from various churches that explain their doctrines and assumptions.

Reading the official Catholic reasoning behind concepts like indulgences, papal infallibility, putative marriages, and annulments can make even a well-educated scholar's head spin. It seems that when churches come across holes or contradictions in previously declared doctrine, they must invent new words, concepts, and assumptions to remedy the situation. Over the centuries, this has made their doctrines and the rationalizations for them extremely complicated.

My analysis is primarily based on teachings from the New Testament, especially quotes of Jesus from the Gospels. I believe that Jesus had, by far, the closest relationship with God while being in the flesh compared with any other person or prophet who has ever lived. As a result, his understanding of God's law exceeded all who preceded him. He had the knowledge and authority to correct misinterpretations in the law that were being practiced at the time.

For instance, Jesus stated, "Moses, because of the hardness of your hearts, permitted you to divorce your wives, but from the beginning it was not so. And I say to you, whoever divorces his wife, except for sexual immorality, and marries another, commits adultery; and whoever marries her who is divorced commits adultery" (Matt 19:8–9). Here, Jesus is instructing us not to follow the teachings of Moses, but instead follow the original way of God, which Jesus was then revealing.

Likewise, in several places in the Old Testament, it is written, "life shall be for life, eye for eye, tooth for tooth" (Lev 24:20; Deut 19:21; Exod 21:24). However, Jesus taught, "You have heard that it was said, 'An eye for an eye and a tooth for a tooth.' But I tell you not to resist an evil person. But whoever slaps you on your right cheek, turn the other to him also" (Matt 5:38–39). Thus, we find different and even contradictory teachings when comparing the Old Testament with the New Testament, even though many scholars use elaborate reasonings and assumptions arguing otherwise.

Typically, I put greatest weight and value in the direct quotes of Jesus from the Gospels, followed by quotes of the apostles, and then other New Testament teachings.

Therefore, most quotes in this book are direct quotes of Jesus from the Gospels or other New Testament writings.

Throughout this book, if I refer to the early churches as a whole or the Catholic Church in particular, I capitalize *Church*. If I do not capitalize *church*, I am indicating Christian churches in general.

The issues of greatest concern, which I discuss in this book, include how churches have effectively reversed the teachings of Jesus regarding adultery, marriage, money, greed, prayer, and idolatry. I will show that the Catholic Church considers itself infallible. I will also demonstrate how it appears that most churches have made their survival and what is good for their organizations more important than the Word of the Lord.

1

History of the Church

FOLLOWING IS A BRIEF summary of the important events throughout history that have shaped the doctrines of churches. Many of the facts presented are from *The Christian Conspiracy: How the Teachings of Christ Have Been Altered by Christians* by Dr. L. David Moore.

Moore demonstrates that the Church made three major decisions in the first few hundred years of its existence: 1) the teachings of the Church must be uniform; 2) these teachings must be based on *apostolic tradition*; and 3) anyone not accepting the uniform teachings of the Church was excluded from Church participation or executed as a heretic.[1]

Apostolic tradition encompasses the doctrines resulting from centuries of debate in the early Church. The Church considers the results of these debates as authoritative as Scripture (i.e., as true as Scripture). These debates occurred mostly in the first five hundred years after Jesus's crucifixion, among men who had never met the apostles. These debates were based solely on the accepted writings about Jesus and the apostles as well as the outcomes of previous debates; thus, when details were lacking, the participants made assumptions.

1. Moore, *Christian Conspiracy*, 122.

These uniform doctrines and teachings of the Church included several definitions regarding the person, nature, and role of Jesus, which is termed *Christology*. This debate has caused more division in the Church than any other topic. By the sixth century, Jesus was defined as the only-begotten Son of God, who was born of the Virgin Mary, and is both completely divine as God and completely human. In chapter 3, I will show that the Church has altered the definition of Christ from that which is presented in Scripture, and that the Church leaders were obsessed with defining Jesus and putting the Lord in a box.

During the first several hundred years of the Church, the Roman emperors wanted uniformity and no conflicts from religious debate within their empire, thus the Church was forced to standardize its theology. Therefore, the Church and the emperor felt the need to define Jesus beyond what the Scriptures say about him.

The ecumenical councils of antiquity were conferences of church leaders and theological experts that were often convened by the emperor. They were held mostly to settle theological debates that were causing controversies within the Church and the empire. Whoever presented a more persuasive argument or whichever reasoning pleased the men in power and supported their viewpoints won the debate. Once an assumption is used in a winning debate and becomes canonical law, it is no longer an assumption; it is considered truth. Many of the doctrines generated during the first few ecumenical councils are still being taught as truth by churches to their congregations today.

- During the First Ecumenical Council in 325 AD, it was determined that priests could not marry even though many disciples were married. The Creed of Nicaea was adopted, which defines Jesus as the only-begotten Son of God, being equal in divinity to God in all ways. The Church would excommunicate anyone who did not agree.

- In 367, the majority of the Church accepted the traditional canon.[2] In other words, by this time, the Church had decided which manuscripts would be included in the Bible and which manuscripts would be excluded and possibly be considered heresy.

- During the Third Ecumenical Council in 431, Mary was declared to be the mother of God.

- At the Fifth Ecumenical Council in 553, Emperor Justinian insisted that the members define the Christ once and for all to stop all of the controversies.

- In 1096, Pope Urban II blessed the First Crusade, which was a military campaign to free the Holy Land of Muslims. Crusaders were not trying to convert Muslims or Jews to save their souls; instead they simply wanted to kill as many of them as possible.[3] The pope promised indulgences to all warriors who participated. He claimed indulgences would wipe away all of their past sins.

- In 1209, Pope Innocent III declared a crusade against the Waldenses, Humiliati, and Cathars. As a result, an army was sent to wipe out and murder these heretics of the Church's doctrine.[4]

- In 1229, canon law forbade lay preaching. The Waldenses violated this and were excommunicated.

- During the Fourteenth Ecumenical Council in 1274 and Seventeenth Ecumenical Council in 1439, it was

2. Moore, *The Christian Conspiracy*, 79.

3. Moore, *Christian Conspiracy*, 99–101.

4. Moore, *The Christian Conspiracy*, 103.

decided that upon death, one's soul would immediately go to heaven, hell, or purgatory.[5]

- In 1302, Pope Boniface VIII required that "for salvation, every creature must be subject to the Roman Pontiff."[6] This was the concept of no salvation outside of the Church (i.e., *extra ecclesiam nulla salus*).

- In 1452, Pope Nicholas V issued an order that legitimized war and slavery on groups that had rejected Christianity.

- In 1478, by official order of Pope Sixtus IV, the Inquisition would report directly to the king and queen of Spain. The monarchs then passed a law that all Moors and Jews must become Christian or they would be put to death or exiled. "Since the Church could not be absolutely certain that these confessed Christians were truly Christian, it had to find out even if it killed those Christians during the discovery process. And of course, when they had been killed by the Inquisition, their property was divided between the Church and the Crown."[7]

- During the fifteenth to seventeenth centuries, Spanish and Portuguese conquistadors murdered fifty million native people.[8] The Church declared that the Americas were bestowed by God to the Spanish and Portuguese. In 1513, the Spanish monarchy issued a declaration called the Requerimiento, which was a statement of Christian faith that the conquistadors read to native tribes to determine if they would accept Christianity. The statement was intentionally read in Spanish or

5. Moore, *Christian Conspiracy*, 97.
6. De Rosa, *Vicars of Christ*, 79.
7. Moore, *Christian Conspiracy*, 104–5.
8. Moore, *Christianity and the New Age Religion*, 112.

Latin, so when the native people could not understand it and walked away in confusion, the conquistadors believed they had the right to attack the tribe, murder the unbelievers, and take their gold/possessions, since they had rejected Christianity.

- In 1484, Pope Innocent IV issued a decree confirming his support for inquisitional proceedings against witches. Some scholars estimate that several million suspected witches were executed by the churches during the fifteenth to eighteenth centuries. "There was absolutely no difference in the way Protestants and Catholics went after witches. Luther and Calvin both advocated torture for producing confessions and recommended that the confessed witches be burned at the stake, just as the Catholics did . . . Many innocent people were executed in the name of a religion which believed it had the right to kill the body in order to save the soul of a sinner."[9]

In this summary of important events in the history of the churches, it is evident that the results of the debates of the first few ecumenical councils generated doctrines that many churches, even today, consider as authoritative as Scripture. This is despite the fact that these debates occurred hundreds of years after Jesus's crucifixion, among men who never met the apostles. It has been shown that the churches continued to create doctrines over the centuries that seem to be contrary to the teachings of Jesus as presented in the Scriptures.

Despite the atrocities that have occurred throughout history resulting from the false assumptions and resulting doctrines of the churches, we find positive changes within many of the churches, especially since the Protestant Reformation. The Reformation brought about a new way of

9. Moore, *Christian Conspiracy*, 108–9.

thinking in which individuals could rely on Scripture as their primary source of belief, instead of exclusively relying on the doctrines of a church.

Even though churches have made many improvements since the Reformation, the information presented in the following chapters reveals that all modern-day churches are far from perfect. Therefore, it is of utmost importance that individuals study Scripture for themselves to discover the true guidance of the Lord.

2

Fallacy of Infallibility

INFALLIBLE MEANS BEING INCAPABLE of making a mistake or an error. The Roman Catholic Church declares before God and humankind that the popes are infallible, which means they have never, or will never, make any errors/mistakes while rendering official decisions for the Church. This includes creating new Church doctrine, declaring rules and guidelines for clergy and parishioners, deciding who is a heretic, determining the punishment for people who break Church rules or who are declared heretics, and so on.

What the Scriptures Say about Infallibility

Papal infallibility is a concept created by the Church over 1,800 years after Jesus's crucifixion. As such, no verses directly address this concept. However, the Scriptures do say that all people sin and make mistakes, which includes the popes.

> For all have sinned, and come short of the glory of God. (Rom 3:23)

> There is none righteous, no, not one. (Rom 3:10)

> For there is not a just man on earth who does good, and does not sin. (Eccl 7:20)

What the Catholic Church Declares about Itself

As previously stated, the Roman Catholic Church declares that the popes have been infallible throughout the Church's history. It makes this claim through extensive arguments and assumptions based on the following two Scriptures: "Whatever you bind on earth will be bound in heaven, and whatever you loose on earth will be loosed in heaven" (Matt 18:18); "He who hears you hears me" (Luke 10:16).

The Church assumes and claims that the pope is the direct successor of the apostle Peter; thus, all authority that Jesus gave to the apostles transfers from pope to pope. How it stretches this to infallibility does not make sense, since even Peter made mistakes, as demonstrated when he denied Jesus.

Regardless of the elaborate rationalizations and assumptions used to make this claim of infallibility, it should be obvious from studying popes' decisions over the course of the Church's history that the claim is simply not true. In many cases throughout history, a pope completely reversed the declarations of a previous pope. Therefore, one of them must have been in error. Many theologies have been declared orthodox by one pope but later declared heretical by a subsequent pope, and vice versa.

In the early fifteenth century, three popes ruled simultaneously, and they excommunicated one another. This alone proves that papal infallibility is simply not true, and rather absurd to claim. Yet the Church continues to put this illusion before the masses, who seem to accept it as truth.

The following are examples of popes reversing or contradicting decisions of previous popes and making "infallible decrees" that seem to contradict the teachings of Jesus as presented in the Gospels:

- In 1854, Pope Pius IX declared that Mary was immaculately conceived (i.e., born free of original sin), which contradicted Pope Gregory I the Great, who declared, "Christ *alone* was conceived without sin."[1]

- Before 1830, the Church insisted that charging interest on a loan was forbidden and doing so could get the lender excommunicated. This decree made sense because it was based on many Scriptures (e.g., Luke 6:35; Deut 23:19; Ps 15:5). In 1830, the Church reversed its position, so it could lend money at interest so long as it wasn't at an "exorbitant rate."[2]

- In 1229, the Decree of the Council of Toulouse forbade the laity from owning or reading the Bible, and in 1713, Pope Clement XI condemned any layperson for reading the Bible.[3] In the fourteenth century, if any laity was caught possessing a Bible, he or she was punished by confiscation of real and personal property, whipping, and burning at the stake.

- In 1252, Pope Innocent IV issued an order permitting the Inquisition to use torture to get a confession of heresy. The punishment was usually burning at the stake, regardless of whether or not the accused confessed.[4]

- In 1536, the Church burned William Tyndale at the stake for translating the Bible into English so that the common person could read it. He received this judgment because the Church forbade anyone outside of clergy from owning or reading the Bible.

1. Moore, *Christian Conspiracy*, 149.
2. Moore, *Christian Conspiracy*, 179.
3. Maitland, *Facts and Documents*, 194.
4. Moore, *Christian Conspiracy*, 104.

- The Church condemned Galileo to house arrest for life for stating that the Earth orbited the Sun, despite there being no Scripture supporting the idea of a heliocentric universe. This was not just a theory Galileo postulated; it was an observation of truth. Galileo could have shown the pope the moons orbiting Jupiter through his telescope, yet the Church would not even look at the evidence.

- For hundreds of years, the Church charged money for indulgences, which it claimed would absolve the purchaser or others from their sins (see chapter 6).

- Jesus said, "Don't address anyone here on earth as Father" (Matt 23:9 NLT), but the Catholic Church requires their parishioners call their clergy "Father" (see chapter 9).

- Church-supported Spanish and Portuguese conquistadors murdered fifty million native people.[5]

- Boniface VIII required that "for salvation, every creature must be subject to the Roman Pontiff."[6]

- In 453, Pope Leo the Great wrote that lay preaching was forbidden. This Church doctrine continued until it was officially reversed by the 1983 revised Code of Canon Law, which explicitly states that laypersons may preach in church.[7]

- Several million suspected witches were executed by both Catholics and Protestants during the last thousand years.

- Pope John XII was killed by a man who had found the pontiff in bed with his wife committing adultery.[8]

5. Moore, *Christianity and the New Age Religion*, 112.

6. De Rosa, *Vicars of Christ*, 79.

7. Parachini, *Lay Preaching*, 10.

8. Tharoor, "7 Wicked Popes," lines 44–46.

- In 1378, Pope Urban VI learned of a conspiracy to remove him from office. He then had six cardinals arrested, tortured, and executed.[9]

- In the eleventh century, Pope Benedict IX resigned and sold the papacy to another priest. Because of his reported licentious behavior, Pope Benedict IX was described by a subsequent pope as having a life "so vile, so foul, so execrable, that I shudder to think of it."[10]

- For hundreds of years, the Church taught that abortion was not murder as long as it was performed within the first forty days for males and eighty days for females.[11] This has obviously been reversed by the Church, and it now considers all intentional abortions murder.

Papal infallibility became official Church doctrine during Vatican I in 1869 and 1870. It was a new concept at the time, not previously taught by the Church. No documentation exists of any Church council before Vatican I mentioning papal infallibility.[12]

When a church believes it cannot make a mistake, something is seriously wrong, since only God is perfect. With such an assumption, a pope cannot admit that previous popes made any mistakes, so they are forced to keep building assumptions and theories based on false beliefs and ideas made in the past. They cannot step back, admit where they went astray, and correct themselves.

As we see in the above decisions and declarations, the Church has much blood on its hands. Yet because it

9. Tharoor, "7 Wicked Popes," lines 50–52.

10. Tharoor, "7 Wicked Popes," lines 54–57.

11. Moore, *Christian Conspiracy*, 213–14.

12. Moore, *Christian Conspiracy*, 151.

maintains its popes have always been and will always be infallible, it will not admit to or repent from its mistakes. As a result, the Church's teachings got bent, a little at a time, by pope after pope, assuming no previous decision was ever in error, until their assumptions and doctrines have completely reversed the teachings of Jesus.

The Catholic, Orthodox, Lutheran, and a few other Protestant churches believe that some or all of the ecumenical councils were infallible. Other churches believe only certain aspects of the first few ecumenical councils were infallible. However, many churches in existence today do not make any claims of infallibility.

3

Christology

WHEN ANALYZING THE GOSPELS in the original language of the New Testament, nowhere does Jesus state that he is divine or that he is the only Son of God,[1] but several hundred years after his crucifixion, the Church insisted that these are facts and anyone who questioned them would be burned at the stake.

What the Scriptures Say about Jesus

In only four places in the New Testament is Jesus called the only Son of God, and he never called himself that in the Bible. Jesus is called the only Son of God in the Gospel of John and the letters of John, which may have all been written by the same author.

In *Christianity and the New Age Religion*, Dr. Moore argues that in the translation from Greek to English, the word *only* was mistranslated from the Greek word *monogenes*, which actually means *unique*. Many biblical scholars agree that in the original Greek, the New Testament does not state that Jesus is the only Son of God.[2]

1. Moore, *Christian Conspiracy*, 6.
2. Moore, *Christian Conspiracy*, 128.

In the New Testament, Jesus teaches that he is not as good or as divine as God:

> Jesus said, "My Father is greater than I." (John 14:28)

> Jesus said, "Why do you call me good? No one is good but one, that is, God." (Mark 10:18)

Therefore, the Scriptures do not state that Jesus is the only Son of God or that he is equivalent to God in divinity. Yet, many churches insist that these are facts.

What Churches Declare about Jesus

The Apostles' Creed, which Catholic parishioners recite during Mass, states, "I believe in Jesus Christ, his only Son, our Lord. He was conceived by the power of the Holy Spirit and born of the Virgin Mary. He suffered under Pontius Pilate, was crucified, died, and was buried. He descended to the dead. On the third day he rose again. He ascended into heaven, and is seated at the right hand of the Father. He will come to judge the living and the dead."

All of what the Apostles' Creed states may be true, but I humbly say that I do not know, for it is not what is written in the Scriptures. Jesus may certainly be the only Son of God, but it is not my place to define God or Jesus. I think only God and Jesus can truly understand their unique relationship. It is not for humans to put God or Jesus in a box. Our job is to obediently follow the Lord's guidance and teachings.

In Mark 14:62, Jesus agrees with Peter that he is the Christ. However, I also choose to stay out of the business of trying to define the Christ. Furthermore, many hypotheses proposed by scholars try to explain what Jesus meant by calling himself "the Son of Man." I do not waste my time with such theories that cannot be proven and are inconsequential for an individual to be an obedient follower of Jesus.

It has been shown that the Church went far beyond what is written in the Bible and defined the following:

- Jesus is the only-begotten Son of God, who was born of Mary, a virgin.

- Mary is the Mother of God, who was immaculately conceived.

- Jesus is both completely as divine as God in all ways and yet completely human.

A lot of what is declared above is not based on Scripture, yet during much of the Church's history, an individual would be excommunicated or burned at the stake for disagreeing with any aspect of it.

Even though the days of burning people at the stake over doctrine have long past, many modern-day churches still insist that the doctrine created during the first few ecumenical councils regarding Christology is truth. This includes the Catholic, Orthodox, Lutheran, and a few other Protestant churches. However, many churches, like the Baptists, rely on what is written in Scripture for their understanding of the person, nature, and role of Jesus.

Defining Jesus and putting the Lord in a box is unnecessary for an individual to be a good Christian. What is important is that an individual "take up his cross" (Matt 16:24) and be an obedient follower of Jesus's teachings. This includes that you "love the Lord your God with all your heart, with all your soul, and with all your mind" (Matt 22:37), "love your neighbor as yourself" (Mark 12:31), "love your enemies" (Matt 5:44), "repent of your sins and turn to God" (Acts 3:19 NLT), "deny [yourself]" (Mark 8:34), "give to the poor" (Matt 19:21), "not commit adultery" (Matt 5:27), "honor your father and your mother" (Matt 15:4), etc.

4

Prayer

Jesus's Instruction on Prayer

Nowhere in the Bible does Jesus say to pray to Mary, the angles, or the saints. In Matthew 6:9, Jesus instructs us to pray to God using the Lord's Prayer. The act of petitioning anyone except God and Jesus through prayer, including Mary or the saints, is against Scripture.

The Church's Instruction on Prayer

It is the official position of the Roman Catholic Church that Catholics do not pray *to* the saints or Mary; instead, they can ask the saints or Mary to pray *for* them. But, in practice, many Catholics do not know this distinction and simply pray to Mary and the saints. Regardless of whether Catholics are praying to Mary and the saints or asking them to pray for them, both practices are against Scripture.

In First Timothy it is written, "For there is one God and *one* mediator between God and men, the man Christ Jesus" (2:5). Since Jesus is the one and only mediator, Mary and the saints cannot mediate for us. Therefore, praying to or petitioning Mary and the saints violates the first commandment: "You shall have no other gods before me" (Exod 20:3).

When churches make statues of Mary, the saints, etc., and then encourage people to pray before them, it is a violation of the next commandment: "Thou shalt not make unto thee any graven image" (Exod 20:4–5 KJV).

Prayer should be all about improving one's personal relationship with God and Jesus. Prayer does not need to be a formal practice done at only certain times or locations. Instead, it should become a part of everything you do. I am frequently asking the Lord for his love, guidance, and protection as I go about my day. It is also important to regularly give thanks to God for the countless blessings he has bestowed upon us all. By keeping the Lord in your thoughts throughout the day, your relationship with him will grow to where he becomes integral to everything you do.

5

Graven Images

A GRAVEN IMAGE IS a statue of anything that is in heaven or earth, including Jesus, Mary, the saints, angles, cherubs, demons, animals, dragons, etc.

What Scripture Says about Graven Images

Thou shalt not make unto thee any graven image, or any likeness of any thing that is in heaven above, or that is in the earth beneath, or that is in the water under the earth. Thou shalt not bow down thyself to them, nor serve them: for I the Lord thy God am a jealous God. (Exod 20:4–5 KJV)

Forasmuch then as we are the offspring of God, we ought not to think that the Godhead is like unto gold, or silver, or stone, graven by art and man's device. (Acts 17:29 KJV)

Little children, keep yourselves from idols. (1 John 5:21)

Therefore, my beloved, flee from idolatry. (1 Cor 10:14)

> Professing to be wise, they became fools, and
> changed the glory of the incorruptible God into
> an image made like corruptible man—and birds
> and four-footed animals and creeping things.
> (Rom 1:22–23)

How Churches Regard Graven Images

With numerous verses throughout the Bible instructing us not to make graven images, it is inconceivable why churches are obsessed with filling their buildings and museums with statues of Jesus, Mary, the saints, and, even more incredibly, dragons, demons, devils, and all kinds of creatures. An Internet search of "Vatican graven images" provides a plethora of graven images the Catholic Church displays and then charges a fee to allow the public to view them, making millions of dollars each year.

Most Catholic churches have prayer stations consisting of a statue of Mary or a saint surrounded by candles, with a kneeling pew in front of it. Catholics put money into the collection slot, light a candle, kneel before the statue, and pray. Many other churches also fill their buildings with statues and images. However, it should be noted that some churches purposefully keep their places of worship free from statues and images because of the Second Commandment.

Neither the Bible nor any other historical records provide firsthand accounts of Jesus's physical appearance before the resurrection. The familiar images of Jesus, Mary, and the apostles commonly depicted in many paintings and statues originated in art from the Byzantine Era, from the fourth century onward. Scholars agree that these images probably have no resemblance to these individuals' appearances.

Even though the secular world classifies many of these statues and paintings as priceless art, a Christian should not value these images and certainly not pray before them. A form created by human hands, especially when it's representation is not accurate, only detracts from the original. Our personal relationship with Jesus is what is important, not valuing a statue of him, which likely does not resemble him at all.

6

Indulgences

THE CATHOLIC CHURCH CLAIMS that an indulgence will reduce the amount of punishment someone experiences after death due to sin. An indulgence is issued by the Church in exchange for a good deed done in this life, which can include donating money to the Church. The indulgence can apply to oneself, or it can be bought for someone else.

What Scripture Says about Indulgences

The Church invented the concept of indulgences about one thousand years after Jesus's crucifixion; therefore, no verses in the Bible address this topic. However, Scripture does state that repentance is required for forgiveness of sin. It says nothing about paying the Church for forgiveness of sin.

> Repent therefore and be converted, that your sins may be blotted out. (Acts 3:19)

> Jesus said, "Unless you repent you will all likewise perish." (Luke 13:3)

Why the Church Invented Indulgences

The Church invented indulgences in the Middle Ages, claiming that an indulgence will provide relief in the after-life from damnation and punishment for sins. They were first widely used during the First Crusade by Pope Urban II, when he granted them to the armed crusaders who were promised immediate salvation if they died while fighting to free the Holy Land from Muslims.

The good deed that indulgences are based upon even-tually changed from giving up one's life to free the Holy Land to simply donating to the Church. As a result, indul-gences became more of a money transaction for forgiveness of sin and were widely abused by the Church for hundreds of years.

Indulgences were a major divisive issue that con-tributed to the Protestant Reformation. As a result, most Protestant churches have never believed in indulgences, and most modern-day churches do not issue them. Fur-thermore, since the Reformation, the Catholic Church has revamped its rules regarding indulgences several times.

I have demonstrated that forgiveness of sin cannot be purchased with money. Instead, it is the free gift of God when you believe in the Lord and repent from your sins.

> God saved you by his grace when you believed. And you can't take credit for this; it is a gift from God. (Eph 2:8 NLT)

> Let the wicked change their ways and banish the very thought of doing wrong. Let them turn to the Lord that he may have mercy on them. Yes, turn to our God, for he will forgive generously. (Isa 55:7 NLT)

7

Churches and Money

What Jesus Says about the Love of Money

> It is easier for a camel to go through the eye of a needle than for a rich man to enter the kingdom of God. (Matt 19:24)

> You cannot serve God and mammon [money/wealth]. (Matt 6:24; Luke 16:13)

> Now the Pharisees, who were lovers of money, also heard all these things, and they derided him. And, he said to them, "You are those who justify yourselves before men, but God knows your hearts. For what is highly esteemed among men is an abomination in the sight of God." (Luke 16:14–15)

> Jesus said, "If you want to be perfect, go, sell what you have and give to the poor, and you will have treasure in heaven; and come, follow me." (Matt 19:21)

What Churches Teach and Do Regarding Money

Peter De Rosa showed that by 1330, the official teaching of the Catholic Church was that Jesus and the apostles did not live lives of poverty. This provided the excuse for clergy to live opulent lifestyles from that day forward.[1]

Even though many clergy have enjoyed living opulent lifestyles since 1330, the current pope, Pope Francis, has made significant steps in trying to reverse this trend in the Church. He has lived a more economical lifestyle compared with most of his predecessors. For instance, he lives in a small suite in the Vatican guesthouse instead of the luxurious Apostolic Palace of the Vatican, which is the typical residence of the pope. Despite his efforts, many reports tell of church leaders living lavish lifestyles. For instance, a German bishop spent $43 million to remodel his luxurious residence, and ten of the top U.S. Catholic Church leaders live in residences worth more than $1 million.[2]

Entry to the Vatican museums and Sistine Chapel costs over 16 euros (about $18 USD). With more than four million visitors per year, the Church receives well over $72 million USD yearly to display their gallery of graven images.

I have focused on the Catholic Church here; however, if you research other Christian churches, many also have opulent buildings, retreats, and headquarters, as well as residences for their clergy.

Despite all of this, it should be noted that the clergy/monastics of some churches and members within some orders of the Catholic Church take a vow of poverty. For instance, Orthodox monks and sisters belonging to the Missionaries of Charity established by Mother Teresa live very economical lifestyles and have dedicated their lives to serving the poorest of the poor.

In this chapter, we have learned that Scripture warns us that loving money and chasing after wealth gets in the way of our relationship with God. We are instructed to put

1. De Rosa, *Vicars of Christ*, 212–13.

2. Burke, "Lavish Homes of Archbishops," lines 6, 14.

God first in our lives and he will take care of our physical needs. "Seek the Kingdom of God above all else, and
live righteously, and he will give you everything you need"
(Matt 6:33 NLT). If God has blessed us with wealth, it is not
for us to hoard it or to live extravagantly, but to use wisely to
care for our families, widows, orphans, and the poor.

8

Call No Man Father

What Jesus Said

Jesus said, "Don't address anyone here on earth as 'Father,' for only God in heaven is your Father." (Matt 23:9 NLT)

What Some Churches Teach Regarding the Lord's Command

THE CATHOLIC, ORTHODOX, ANGLICAN, and certain Lutheran churches instruct their congregations to call their clergy "Father."

These churches offer plenty of assumptions and rationalizations, but why blatantly defy Jesus's clear instruction? Churches have a long history of inventing words to suit their doctrines, and one wonders why they did not just invent a word for their clergy instead of doing exactly what Jesus said not to do.

Wouldn't humility before God and simple respect of Jesus's command be the best approach? When the Church first started this practice, its leaders must have known about this scripture, yet they ignored it and established that their clergy were to be called "Father." Doing so seems to me to be testing the Lord, which makes no sense at all. As a result, all churches other than the ones listed above have chosen to call their clergy by other titles like pastor, elder, reverend, bishop, or president.

If you belong to a church that calls their clergy "Father," I encourage you to join me in praying for the church leaders to contemplate God's Word, follow all of Jesus's instructions for themselves, and lead their congregations to do likewise.

9

Marriage and Adultery

THE FOLLOWING IS BY far the longest chapter in this book. This is because adultery is the most complex and least understood of all sins. Critical information describing when a relationship is adultery and how to repent from adultery is missing from the Bible.

This chapter is also, in my opinion, the most important chapter in this book. Other chapters in this book discuss things that church leaders have done that go against the teachings of Jesus as described in Scripture. As a result, it is the church leaders' souls that may be at risk when they do things like live lavish lifestyles. Whereas this chapter deals with a very serious sin that the churches teach their followers is not a sin, so it is their followers' souls that may be in jeopardy when they believe and act upon the false assumptions and teachings of the churches.

A large percentage of modern Christians do not know what the Bible says on many issues because they have blindly followed their churches' teachings without ever studying the Bible in depth for themselves. In particular, many are not aware that the New Testament clearly and consistently states that a woman is bound by the law of God as long as her husband lives. It does not matter whether she divorces her husband or if her husband divorces her. Neither does it matter what reasons either spouse gives to justify divorce.

According to Scripture, after a divorce or separation, a woman must continue to live as though she is still married until her husband dies. Any romantic or physical relationship she enters into while her husband is alive may very well be adultery. According to Scripture, once her husband dies, she is free from God's law regarding her husband and may remarry.

These instructions may seem male-chauvinistic to a modern-day reader of Scripture; however, with humility, open-mindedness, and persistence in studying Scripture, an individual will come to understand why such laws are good for humankind and are truly divinely inspired. Furthermore, I will show later in this chapter that the instructions given in the Gospels regarding marriage and divorce are equally stringent for both husbands and wives.

Despite what the Gospels say, almost every church in existence today seems to ignore them and celebrates, condones, and encourages what Jesus says are adulterous unions, which refers to many, if not most, second marriages after divorce. As a result, many couples enter into second marriages not knowing that it is adultery. In fact, many people do not realize how serious the sin of adultery is and that it should be avoided at all cost. According to Scripture, adultery is extremely destructive to one's soul.

The teachings of Jesus in the Bible regarding married men are not as complete as they are for women, and a crucial inconsistency exists in the Gospels regarding marriage and divorce for men. There is only one place in the entire New Testament where Jesus *may* have said that a man who remarries after he divorces his wife for infidelity does not commit adultery. This is in the Gospel of Matthew. However, this same teaching, at the same time and place in Jesus's life, is also documented in the Gospel of Mark, and it contradicts the account in Matthew. This inconsistency may mean that a husband should choose not to remarry after a divorce until his wife dies, no matter the circumstances.

Jesus's Definition of Adultery and When Remarriage after Divorce Is Permitted

The New Testament teaches strongly and consistently that marriage should be a lifelong commitment. The following is the only verse in the entire Bible in which Jesus *may* have said that remarriage for a man after he divorces his wife for infidelity is not a sin: "And I say to you, whoever divorces his wife, except for sexual immorality, and marries another, commits adultery; and whoever marries her who is divorced commits adultery" (Matt 19:9).

In only one other verse, interestingly also in the Gospel of Matthew, Jesus states something similar: "But I say to you that whoever divorces his wife for any reason except sexual immorality causes her to commit adultery; and whoever marries a woman who is divorced commits adultery" (5:32).

Notice that this verse says nothing about whether it is permitted for a man to remarry after divorce. It only states that if he divorces his wife for infidelity, he is not responsible for her subsequent adultery.

According to this verse, if a man divorces his wife for any reason other than infidelity and she remarries, that remarriage is adulterous, and the husband who divorced her is liable for her adultery. In other words, this scripture says that a husband is responsible to keep his wife from becoming an adulteress by protecting the marriage the best he can. It has nothing to do with instructing a man about when it is okay for him to remarry, even after his wife commits adultery and they divorce.

As stated above, Matthew 19:9 is the only verse in the entire Bible in which Jesus *may* have said that it would not be adultery if a man remarried after divorcing his wife for infidelity. Jesus said these words when he entered into Judea and the Pharisees challenged him (see Matt 19:1–3).

This same event was recorded in the Gospel of Mark, which was written over a decade before the Gospel of Matthew, according to a majority of scholars. We know that it was the same event because Mark 10:1–2 mentions that Jesus entered Judea and the Pharisees challenged him. This scripture reads: "Whoever divorces his wife, and marries another, commits adultery against her. And, if a woman divorces her husband and marries another, she commits adultery" (Mark 10:11–12).

This verse indicates that in all cases if a man divorces his wife and remarries, he commits adultery. Even if a husband does nothing wrong, and his wife commits adultery and divorces him, he does not have permission to remarry. This is certainly not the same as the Matthew account. Furthermore, the Gospel of Luke seems to match Mark's account rather than Matthew's: "Whoever divorces his wife and marries another commits adultery; and whoever marries her who is divorced from her husband commits adultery" (Luke 16:18).

As mentioned previously, all teachings in the New Testament consistently state that a woman must not remarry while her husband is alive, no matter the circumstances. The scriptures given above are consistent in this manner. Following are a couple more examples:

> For the woman who has a husband is bound by the law to her husband as long as he lives. But if the husband dies, she is released from the law

of her husband. So then if, while her husband lives, she marries another man, she will be called an adulteress; but if her husband dies, she is free from that law, so that she is no adulteress, though she has married another man. (Rom 7:2–3)

A wife is bound by law as long as her husband lives. (1 Cor 7:39)

It should be obvious to serious students of the Bible that adultery is nothing a Christian should ever even consider committing. Some churches declare that all sins are equally bad for the soul, while others say adultery is a mortal sin, which is much worse than most other sins. A mortal sin is one that some churches say is a gravely sinful act that can lead to damnation if the person does not repent from it before he or she dies. Scripture does provide evidence that certain sins are more destructive to one's soul than others:

All unrighteousness is sin, and there is sin not leading to death. (1 John 5:17)

Whoever therefore breaks one of the least of these commandments, and teaches men so, shall be called least in the kingdom of heaven. (Matt 5:19)

These quotations demonstrate the severity of adultery:

Whoever commits adultery with a woman lacks understanding; he who does so destroys his own soul. (Prov 6:32)

Flee sexual immorality. Every sin that a man does is outside the body, but he who commits sexual immorality sins against his own body. (1 Cor 6:18)

Because they are adulteresses, and blood is on their hands. (Ezek 23:45)

> God is my witness: one adultery is as bad as many murders; and what is terrible in it is this, that the fearfulness and impiety of its murders are not seen. For, when blood is shed, the dead body remains lying, and all are struck by the terrible nature of the occurrence. But the murders of the soul caused by adultery, though they are more frightful, yet, since they are not seen by men, do not make the daring a whit less eager in their impulse. Know, O man, whose breath it is that thou hast to keep thee in life, and thou shalt not wish that it be polluted. By adultery alone is the breath of God polluted. And therefore it drags him who has polluted it into the fire; for it hastens to deliver up its insulter to everlasting punishment. (the apostle Peter, from the *Clementine Homilies*)[1]

This last quotation is not from the Bible but from writings that several early Christian theologians referenced. It is a good description of how the apostle Peter may have viewed the severity of adultery. Recall that John the Baptist was imprisoned and subsequently executed because he stated in public that Herod's marriage was adulterous. If Jesus, John the Baptist, the apostle Peter, and other early Christians considered adultery to be such a grave sin, why do modern-day churches celebrate adultery in the name of the Lord?

One of the most controversial stories in the New Testament is the story of the woman caught in adultery. Here Jesus *may* have said, "He who is without sin among you, let him throw a stone at her first" (John 8:7). The earliest manuscripts of the Gospel of John do not contain this story. However, manuscripts written after about the beginning of the fifth century include this story. The majority of scholars

1. Roberts and Donaldson, eds., *Ante-Nicene Library, Vol.* 17, 1:222.

believe this event was not originally a part of the Gospel of John. One must wonder, who added it to the Gospel of John centuries after the crucifixion of Jesus, and why?

Finally, what instruction does the New Testament give to a woman who is not happy in her marriage? The answer is given in 1 Corinthians: "A wife is not to depart from her husband. But even if she does depart, let her remain un-married or be reconciled to her husband. And, a husband is not to divorce his wife" (7:10–11). There are no details given in the New Testament regarding how to repent from adultery. As a result, the churches believe it has been their duty to fill in the missing details with their doctrines.

What Churches Teach and Do Regarding Adultery and Remarriage after Divorce

Various churches treat adultery and remarrying in many different ways. I know of only one church group, the Amish, who under all circumstances do not celebrate or condone what Jesus says is adultery in the New Testament. Other churches maintain one of three rationalizations to justify their clergy preforming, condoning, and celebrating a mar-riage that the Gospels say is an adulterous union:

- It is not adultery because Jesus died on the cross to forgive sins. In other words, Jesus's dying on the cross supersedes his teachings and the law of God given in the Scriptures.

- The church simply overrules or rationalizes away the details of Scripture, assuming that the Bible has errors in it or is missing information. In the case of missing information, one church has invented a concept called *Bible principles*, which rationalizes circumstances, not mentioned in the Bible, where a woman is no longer bound by the law of God even though her husband lives.

• The marriage has been proven null and void by the Church based on criteria it has established. Thus, the participants are free to remarry.

Forgiveness of Sins Rationalization

Clergy from some churches will officiate any marriage they are asked to perform based on the fact that Jesus died on the cross for forgiveness of sins. Furthermore, these churches are promising and guaranteeing that what Jesus identified in the Gospels as adulterous unions are equivalent to lawful marriages in every way. However, God's mercy regarding forgiveness of sin does not make continuing the sin acceptable to God or beneficial to one's soul. Forgiveness of sin requires first leaving the sin and then repenting, turning away, from the sin.

If someone enters into a union that Jesus says is adulterous, the participants may end up perpetually committing adultery without ever truly repenting from the sin. How do they ever leave the sin of adultery and truly repent from it if they are convinced that the adultery is now a lawful marriage? Since adulterous unions have the appearance of a legitimate marriage in our society, it has become a way to cover up the sin of adultery without ever truly repenting from the sin. "He who covers his sins will not prosper, but whoever confesses and forsakes them will have mercy" (Prov 28:13).

Oftentimes in these situations, people are convinced that the mistake/sin was the first marriage (also known as the covenant marriage). So they "repent" from the first marriage and pray to God that they are truly sorry for marrying their first spouse. In their ignorance and arrogance, they "repented" by forgiving God for making the mistake of yoking their first marriage together and for putting boundaries on man and woman, which adulterers do not like. The only problem with this "repentance" is that the first marriage was never a sin, for God does not participate in sin when he did the action of yoking the covenant marriage together, and the "solution" to their problem (i.e., the adulterous union) is and always will be a grave sin.

> For this reason a man shall leave his father and mother and be joined to his wife, and the two shall become one flesh. So then, they are no longer two but one flesh. Therefore, what God has yoked together, let not man separate. (Matt 19:5–6)

> When you make a vow to God, do not delay to pay it; for He has no pleasure in fools. Pay what you have vowed—better not to vow than to vow and not pay. (Eccl 5:4–5)

A union identified by Jesus in the Gospels as adultery is not equivalent to a lawful marriage, yet the churches promise otherwise. When the churches declare that these unions are equivalent to covenant marriages, they are effectively teaching the participants that it would be a sin to leave these adulterous unions and the associated perpetual adultery.

To confuse the situation even further, sometimes churches will establish that one of the spouses is the innocent victim in the marriage that is failing or has ended in divorce. This somehow rationalizes that the victim is now free to remarry after the divorce, regardless of the circumstances or whether it is the husband or the wife who is declared the victim.

Bible Principles Rationalization

Some churches have invented words, concepts, doctrines, and procedures that they insist turn what Jesus identified as adulterous unions into legitimate marriages. One church has invented something called *Bible principles*, which goes beyond what is written in the Scriptures and effectively reverses the teachings of Jesus. One such *Bible principle* states that at the moment a woman commits the physical act of adultery, she is released from her marriage and is no longer "bound by law as long as her husband lives" (Rom 7:2; 1 Cor 7:39).

Therefore, all that a married woman needs to do to get out of her unwanted marriage is to commit adultery, divorce her husband, get rebaptized into this special church, and give the church 10 percent of her income for the rest of her life. This church then guarantees that not only is she free to remarry but also that she is not sinning if she does. In fact, it teaches that it would be a sin to leave the adulterous union because it claims that the union is equivalent in every way to a legitimate marriage.

This church did not invent this "principle" based on Scripture; instead, it came about because of its desire to make the church and its members appear as if they are the Lord's only true believers. Any adultery in their congregation is intolerable, so it must be taken care of immediately.

This church is notorious for making outward appearances of utmost importance. Its followers must dress formally for church, keep their houses and yards clean and tidy, etc. Jesus had this same issue with the church/synagogue of his day: "Now you Pharisees make the outside of the cup and dish clean, but your inward part is full of greed and wickedness" (Luke 11:39).

Annulment Rationalization

The Catholic Church has taken a different approach to permitting second marriages. It invented the concept of annulment, which allows it to skirt the problem of its members wanting second marriages despite the teachings of Jesus in the Gospels. An annulment, or formally a "declaration of nullity," is not the dissolution of a marriage but merely a formal finding that a valid marriage was never contracted.

The Catholic Church has consistently held that after a valid marriage is willfully entered into and consummated by two baptized Christians, it is indissoluble until the death of one spouse. However, throughout history certain situations have brought up the question of whether a marriage was valid in the first place, such as when a man kidnaps a young girl and forces her to marry him against her will; or when an individual commits fraud to get another person to agree to marry; or in cases of bigamy, mental incapacity, or lunacy. For these extreme cases, the Church devised the concept of annulment. Gradually, over time, annulment has evolved from being used only in extreme cases to being used to get out of marriages that are simply no longer wanted.

One only needs to convince the Church that some impediment or defect existed in the marriage at the time of the union that would render the marriage contract invalid from the outset. It is usually considered retroactive, meaning that an annulled marriage is considered invalid from the beginning, almost as if it had never taken place.

Once the Church began granting annulments, it created a new dilemma for itself and its doctrines. What happens to children who were born from a marriage that was subsequently annulled? At the moment the annulment is granted, instantly the once-legitimate children become bastards. The Church fixed this contradiction in its doctrine by inventing another new phrase and concept, which it called "putative marriage."

The Church defines a putative marriage as a marriage that was entered into in good faith on the part of at least one of the partners and appeared to be a legitimate marriage at the time. However, at a later time it is found to be invalid due to some impediment or defect in the union. Once the Church determines that a marriage is a putative marriage, it simply declares the children legitimate. Problem solved!

It is quite possible that even though annulments seem to be justified from a human perspective, especially in the extreme cases, there is no scriptural basis for them. God, who does not think like humans, may not agree with the annulments of the Church. Therefore, what the Church condones, participates in, and celebrates may be nothing more than adultery.

It is interesting to note that a major Catholic translation of the Bible, the New American Bible (Revised Edition), has changed the Gospel of Matthew to match this invented doctrine of the Church:

> Whoever divorces his wife (unless the marriage is unlawful) causes her to commit adultery, and whoever marries a divorced woman commits adultery. (Matt 5:32 NABRE)

> Whoever divorces his wife (unless the marriage is unlawful) and marries another commits adultery. (Matt 19:9 NABRE)

In every other major English translation of the Bible, "unless the marriage is unlawful" is not used. Instead, those translations say except for "adultery," "sexual immorality," "fornication," or "marital unfaithfulness."

Repentance from Adultery

The rationalizations discussed above, which are used to condone adulterous unions, are not based on Scripture. Instead, they seem to have evolved from the desire of adulterers to make their sin acceptable to society, church, and God; and from the churches' need to accommodate the desires of their congregants (i.e., to keep their pews and coffers full) while making the whole thing appear acceptable to God. The problem is that it may simply be adultery.

As churches condone divorce and remarriage, it has become a socially acceptable way to cover the transgression without ever repenting from the sin of adultery upon the covenant marriage. True repentance requires first leaving the sinful act forever. Thus, by condoning and celebrating what Jesus says in the Scriptures is adultery, churches may very well be leading their parishioners and congregants into adulterous unions that prevent the participants from ever truly repenting. Instead, it keeps them in a state of perpetual adultery. Practicing adulterers are not allowed into the kingdom of God: "Do not be deceived. Neither fornicators, nor idolaters, nor adulterers, nor homosexuals, nor sodomites, nor thieves, nor covetous, nor drunkards, nor revilers, nor extortioners will inherit the kingdom of God" (1 Cor 6:9–10).

The Scriptures seem to indicate that it does not matter if the participants think (based on false assumptions) that they have repented from adultery or whether the churches say so. It is the judgment of God that matters. True repentance requires stopping the sinful action and changing one's thinking that the sin was or is ever acceptable.

It should be obvious from studying Jesus's teachings in Matthew 5:32; 19:9; Mark 10:11–12; and Luke 16:18 that he clearly defined for humankind what is an adulterous union and what is a legitimate marriage. Despite these teachings from Jesus and his classifying certain unions as adulterous, churches insist that these unions are

- not adulterous,
- equivalent in every way to a lawful marriage, and
- acceptable to God, beneficial to the souls of all involved, and a sin to leave the union.

How do individuals stop the sin of adultery and repent once they have convinced themselves and their social group that they are legitimately remarried? It is as if the second marriage becomes a trap, keeping them locked in a situation of perpetual adultery, where they cannot stop the action in order to properly repent from a grave sin that may lead to the destruction of their souls.

Although modern churches have dismissed or rationalized away this issue, it seems to have concerned the early Church leaders. Ancient manuscripts document their concern about second marriages because they "block repentance." The concept of second marriages blocking repentance is illustrated in *The Shepard of Hermas* (see the appendix).

Because Scripture consistently teaches that a woman is bound by the law of God as long as her husband lives, and there exists seemingly contradictory verses regarding Jesus's teachings about whether it is permissible for a man to remarry after a divorce, it might be best for both divorced men and women not to remarry until after their spouses die, which is what is instructed in *The Shepard of Hermas*.

In the time of Jesus, people were routinely stoned to death if found committing adultery. A real concern existed among early Christians about avoiding this sin and keeping it out of the Christian community. This is a very different mindset from our modern society in which divorce and adultery are commonplace and almost every church condones and celebrates what Jesus taught is adultery.

Churches seem to have no problem going beyond what is written in the Scriptures in order to create black-and-white doctrines that suit the desires of their congregations. This is despite the warning given in the New Testament: "not to go beyond what is written" (1 Cor 4:6 NLT).

I hope I have demonstrated the seriousness of adultery and that Christians who care about their salvation should never consider it. We've seen that almost every church in existence condones and celebrates what Jesus says in the Gospels are adulterous unions. Since the Scriptures instruct us not to enter into adulterous unions, it provides no instructions on how to repent from this sin once an individual finds him- or herself in a marriage that is classified as adulterous. Therefore, take care of and fight for your covenant marriage so you do not end up in this situation.

10

Purpose of Churches

As I STATED IN the introduction, I have no desire to see the churches closed down, since they do provide an important function for humankind. Churches offer a mechanism where the community of faithful can gather to worship, pray, discuss Scripture, share Communion, support one another, and assist the needy. Furthermore, it is one of the best ways of introducing people to Christianity.

What the New Testament Says about Gathering in Jesus's Name

Jesus said, "For where two or three are gathered together in My name, I am there in the midst of them." (Matt 18:20)

When you meet together, one will sing, another will teach, another will tell some special revelation God has given, one will speak in tongues, and another will interpret what is said. But everything that is done must strengthen all of you. (1 Cor 14:26 NLT)

What Is Happening
in the Modern-Day Churches?

Oftentimes, when Christians dedicate themselves to a particular church body for a long period of time, they gain a certain pride about their chosen church. They come to believe that their church is the one that most accurately teaches the truth about God, Jesus, sin, and repentance.

But as we've seen in this brief look at the churches throughout history, all churches are far from perfect. No one should blindly follow them. An in-depth understanding of Scripture provides the knowledge and wisdom needed for individuals to surpass the false doctrines and assumptions churches have taught over the last two thousand years and discover the true teachings of Jesus.

When watching the modern-day popes interact with the crowds of followers, it seems as if Catholics consider their Church leaders to be beyond human and actually worship them by bowing before them and kissing their rings. This is happening despite the following Scripture: "As Peter was coming in, Cornelius met him and fell down at his feet and worshiped him. But Peter lifted him up, saying, 'Stand up; I myself am also a man'" (Acts 10:25–26).

It is as if these huge crowds of followers believe the mass delusion proclaimed by the Church that the pope is infallible and thus beyond human, which has been shown to be a false assumption. The pope sometimes appears to be more like a celebrity who runs a multibillion-dollar corporation instead of being a humble follower of Jesus.

It seems as if churches have replaced the Word of the Lord when it suits their agendas. Many church leaders seem more interested in what is good for their churches and the financial survival of their organizations. What happens when churches continue to condone and participate in adultery, greed, idolatry, arrogance before the Lord, and other sins? Could this explain why many church organizations and leaders continue to be involved in so many modern-day atrocities?

The extent of the sex abuse scandals in the Catholic Church appear to be more than just a coincidence of isolated incidents; rather, it seems to be a systemic problem within the Church. Protestants also seem to have had several prominent pastors involved with modern-day scandals and atrocities. For example:

- A survey of priests, non-ordained brothers and sisters, and other church personnel employed between 1950 and 2009 by the Australian Catholic Church revealed that they were accused of 4,444 child sex abuse incidents over that period of time.[1]

- Research carried out in the United States found that from 1950 through June 2015, 6,500 of the 116,153 Catholic priests who worked during that time have been accused of child sexual abuse.[2]

- Over the last few decades, many Protestant pastors have been accused of, confessed to, or were convicted of cheating on their wives; having sex with minors; being involved with fraud, rape, or illegal drugs; or engaging with prostitutes. An Internet search of "fallen pastors" provides an extensive list of Protestant pastors that have been involved in scandals.

- Recently it was discovered that at least 547 boys at a German Catholic choir school suffered sexual and/or physical abuse in what victims have likened to "prison, hell and a concentration camp."[3]

1. Blumer, "Child Sex Abuse Commission," lines 6–11.
2. Blumer, "Child Sex Abuse Commission," lines 21–23.
3. Dwyer, "Nearly 550 Choirboys Abused," lines 3–5.

Perhaps the atrocities that have plagued the churches throughout history up to the present day, along with the problems discussed in this book, were prophesied long ago in the New Testament:

> There will be false teachers among you, who will secretly bring in destructive heresies . . . And many will follow their destructive ways. (2 Pet 2:1–2)

> Shepherd the church of God which He purchased with His own blood. For I know this, that after my departure savage wolves will come in among you, not sparing the flock. Also from among yourselves men will rise up, speaking misleading things, to draw away the disciples after themselves. (Acts 20:28–30)

> Beware of false prophets, who come to you in sheep's clothing, but inwardly they are ravenous wolves. (Matt 7:15)

I am not stating that all churches are entirely infected with sin and false prophets, but there appears to be serious consequences resulting from the apparent false assumptions and resulting doctrines made up and taught by the churches. This has resulted in a significant percentage of their clergy having fallen into very serious sin. Therefore, my advice to Christians is not to blindly follow the teachings of any church or clergy. Instead, form your foundation of faith based on the truth and wisdom gained through studying the Scriptures and praying to God.

Hope in the Word

DESPITE ALL OF THE problems addressed in this book, there is real hope for us all in the Word of the Lord. As I stated in the introduction, the quotes of Jesus in the Gospels form the basis of my faith. I find these teachings to be fundamentally consistent, and I consider Jesus's authority supreme. Therefore, I implore every Christian to study the New Testament, especially the Gospels, seriously and regularly. I find that I learn something new every time I read through the New Testament.

What the New Testament Says about the Words and Teachings of Jesus

In the beginning was the Word, and the Word was with God, and the Word was God. He was in the beginning with God. All things were made through Him, and without Him nothing was made that was made. In Him was life, and the life was the light of men. And the light shines in the darkness, and the darkness did not comprehend it. (John 1:1–5)

This is My beloved Son, in whom I am well
pleased. Hear Him! (Matt 17:5; Mark 9:7; Luke
9:35; Matt 3:17)

How to Begin Your Personal Journey into Scripture

I have been asked on more than one occasion to share the
techniques I use to study Scripture. The first consideration
is which translation of the Bible most accurately depicts the
true teachings of Jesus.

There are well over fifty popular English translations
of the Bible, and they can vary greatly for a given verse. This
is because they differ on which ancient manuscripts were
used in the translation, the languages of the translated manuscripts, and whether it is more or less a literal translation.

The ancient manuscripts that most English translations of the Bible are based upon were written in Greek, He-
brew, Aramaic, or Latin. A literal translation means that it
is almost a word-for-word translation, whereas a less literal
translation is more of a thought-for-thought translation.

A thought-for-thought translation takes the translator's assumptions and interpretations from several verses in
a manuscript and translates it into English as one copasetic
thought. As a result, the translator can miss the original
intended meaning of the text, and the reader will have no
knowledge that this has occurred. Despite this disadvantage, thought-for-thought translations, due to their readability, are usually recommended for individuals who are
new to reading the Bible.

A literal or word-for-word translation can preserve
the oftentimes subtle meanings and concepts within the
original text, but it can also be very difficult to read and understand. This is because the sentence structure of modern

English is very different from the sentence structures of the ancient languages of the translated manuscripts.

My preference is to seek the original intention of a translated scripture at the expense of the readability of the verse, so I typically read more literal translations of the Bible. My two favorites are the King James Version (KJV) and the New King James Version (NKJV).

In 1604, King James tasked forty-seven scholars of the Church of England to create a new English translation of the Bible, which resulted in the King James Version. It took the forty-seven scholars eight years to accomplish this task. The King James Version was first published in 1611 and has been considered the standard English translation for hundreds of years.

The major disadvantage of the King James Version is that it is written in Elizabethan English, which can be difficult to read, much less understood. As a result, the New King James Version was created and published in 1982. This version is primarily based off of the King James Version but replaces much of the Elizabethan English with modern English. One disadvantage of both of these translations is that they are only based on manuscripts known in the early seventeenth century. Manuscripts discovered since then are not incorporated. Most of the quotes in *Beware of Hypocrisy* are from the New King James Version.

For a more in-depth analysis of the New Testament, I recommend *The New Greek-English Interlinear New Testament*, which contains a literal word-for-word English translation of the Greek text in interlinear form. Thus, you can trace each English word or phrase back to the original Greek. In addition, a parallel column of the New Revised Standard Version (NRSV) accompanies the interlinear text.

Many Bible scholars use Bible dictionaries and concordances when researching the Bible. A Bible concordance is an alphabetical index of the important English words used in the Bible, which gives every location in the Bible where each word is used. Before the computer era, this was the only way in which an individual could easily find all occurrences of a given word in the Bible. A Bible dictionary is simply an English dictionary of many of the words used in the Bible. Both of these resources may be helpful in your Bible studies; however, nowadays, Internet searches and Bible apps can get you the same information much quicker.

In my studies of Scripture, I primarily use Internet searches, online Bibles, and Bible apps to search the Bible and find the definitions of words in both the original text and the translated text. Furthermore, these apps and websites allow you to easily switch between Bible translations to do a side-by-side comparison of different translations of a verse. Since the various translations of the Bible can vary greatly, this is very useful when trying to determine the true meaning of the original text.

For online Bibles, I recommend biblegateway.com. For Bible apps, I recommend YouVersion. Both of these are free and offer the Bible translations in many languages. The YouVersion app works without a network connection for certain translations and is also an audio Bible.

Conclusion

BEWARE OF HYPOCRISY HAS shown that much of the doctrines churches have invented over the last two thousand
years go beyond what is written in Scripture and sometimes
outright contradicts the teachings of Jesus as documented
in the New Testament. We have learned that the churches
and many of their leaders have committed horrible atrocities throughout history up to the present. Furthermore, the
Catholic Church has made it impossible to admit to its past
mistakes and assumptions, much less correct them. It arro-
gantly insists that papal infallibility is and always has been
the truth.

In this short treatise, I have shown that throughout
history, churches seem to participate in and condone sin;
therefore, they should not be relied upon as an individual's
primary source for seeking the truth about God, Jesus, sin,
and repentance. It is crucial for individuals to study the
Scriptures for themselves so they can gain accurate knowledge of the teachings of Jesus.

Only the pure Word of the Lord provides truth, which
is necessary when facing challenges and temptations in life.
Without knowing and understanding Scripture, people are
too easily convinced by a church's doctrine that may not be

based on God's Word. Furthermore, acting on these false assumptions could lead to the damnation of their souls.

It is my heart's desire that this book encourages you to pick up the New Testament and read it in its entirety. Study the Gospels in depth. With the knowledge you gain, I hope you will thoughtfully question what churches are teaching and continually seek to understand the way God wants you to live your life. I pray that churches will repent and turn away from any false assumptions and doctrines they have made and teach.

We are here to maintain and improve our relationship with God. Sin separates us from him in ways that are complex, profound, and not fully understood. Live with a passion to please the Lord, seek his truth, and do what is good. Avoid sin because it pollutes your mind (i.e., mental illnesses), hurts your soul, causes diseases,[1] interferes with your relationship with God, and hurts others more than we can imagine.

Behold, I send you out as sheep in the midst of wolves. Therefore be wise as serpents and innocent as doves.

MATTHEW 10:16

1. Jesus spoke the following after healing a man who could not walk and who had an infirmity for thirty-eight years: "See, you have been made well. Sin no more, lest a worse thing come upon you" (John 5:14). This gives scriptural evidence that sin causes diseases.

Appendix

The Shepherd of Hermas

THE SHEPHERD OF HERMAS was written sometime within the late first to mid second century and was popular among early Christians. It was discovered bound in at least two surviving ancient codices (books) of the New Testament. Some of the early church fathers, such as Irenaeus, considered it to be canonical Scripture.[1]

The Shepherd of Hermas contains the following exchange between Hermas and the Angel of Repentance:[2]

Hermas: "Sir, if any one has a wife who trusts in the Lord, and if he detect[s] her in adultery, does the man sin if he continue[s] to live with her?"

Angel of Repentance: "As long as he remains ignorant of her sin, the husband commits no transgression in living with her. But if the husband know[s] that his wife has gone astray, and if the woman does not repent, but persists in her fornication, and yet the husband continues to live with her, he also is guilty of her crime, and a sharer in her adultery."

1. Davidson and Leaney, *Biblical Criticism*, 230.
2. Roberts and Donaldson, *Ante-Nicene Library*, Vol. 1 1:352–53.

Hermas: "What then, sir, is the husband to do, if his wife continue[s] in her vicious practices?"

Angel of Repentance: "The husband should put her away, and remain by himself. But if he put[s] his wife away and marry another, he also commits adultery."

Hermas: "What if the woman put away should repent, and wish to return to her husband: shall she not be taken back by her husband?"

Angel of Repentance: "Assuredly. If the husband do[es] not take her back, he sins, and brings a great sin upon himself; for he ought to take back the sinner who has repented. But not frequently. For there is but one repentance to the servants of God. In case, therefore, that the divorced wife may repent, the husband ought not to marry another, when his wife has been put away. In this matter man and woman are to be treated exactly in the same way."

About the Author

RAISED IN ROLLING MEADOWS and Buffalo Grove, Illinois, Dr. Robert Waligurski received his Bachelor of Science in physics from the University of Illinois in Champaign/Urbana, Illinois. He received his Master of Science in mechanical engineering from the University of Southern California. He continued his education at the University of Southern California, receiving an EME in controls engineering with a minor in complex systems architecting and a PhD in mechanical engineering.

Over the last thirty years, Dr. Waligurski has worked as a scientist/engineer at the Los Alamos National Laboratory, Hughes Aircraft Company, Boeing Satellite Systems, Boeing Commercial Airplanes, Zodiac Aerospace, and Safran. He has held faculty positions at Chapman University College and Embry-Riddle Aeronautical University.

Dr. Waligurski was a founding board member of the Anacortes Family Center (a shelter for homeless women and children) and was key in achieving funding for and constructing the facility. He was a board member of the organization for over ten years and held the offices of president, treasurer, and secretary.

Rob lives in Washington State in a small town on an island near the Canadian border. He spends much of his free time hiking, biking, and snowboarding in the beautiful Pacific Northwest. He has been a vegetarian since 1998. Rob often snowboards during the winter throughout the Pacific Northwest and even throughout the summer on Mount Hood in Oregon.

Dr. Waligurski has spent over twenty years researching the Bible and ancient manuscripts, seeking the truth about Jesus and his teachings. His passion is to seek and uncover the truth about God, Jesus, humankind, and reality.

Bibliography

Blumer, Clare, et al. "Child Sex Abuse Royal Commission: Data Reveals Extent of Catholic Allegations." *ABC News Australia*, February 7, 2017. http://www.abc.net.au/news/2017-02-06/child-sex-abuse-royal-commission:-data-reveals-catholic-abuse/8243890.

Burke, Daniel. "The Lavish Homes of American Archbishops." *Cable News Network*, August 2014. http://www.cnn.com/interactive/2014/08/us/american-archbishops-lavish-homes/index.html.

Davidson, Robert, and A. R. C. Leaney. *Biblical Criticism.* Harmondsworth, UK: Penguin, 1970.

De Rosa, Peter. *Vicars of Christ: The Dark Side of the Papacy.* New York: Crown, 1988.

Dwyer, Colin. "Nearly 550 German Choirboys Abused at Renowned Catholic School, Report Says." *National Public Radio*, July 19, 2017. https://www.npr.org/sections/thetwo-way/2017/07/19/538103579/nearly-550-german-choir-boys-abused-at-renowned-catholic-school-report-says.

Maitland, Samuel R. *Facts and Documents Illustrative of the History, Doctrine, and Rites, of the Ancient Albigenses & Waldenses.* London: Rivington, 1832.

Moore, L. David. *The Christian Conspiracy: How the Teachings of Christ Have Been Altered by Christians.* Atlanta: Pendulum Plus, 1994.

———. *Christianity and the New Age Religion: A Bridge Toward Mutual Understanding.* Atlanta: Pendulum Plus, 1992.

Parachini, Patricia A. *Lay Preaching: State of the Question.* Collegeville, MN: Liturgical, 1940.

Roberts, Alexander, and James Donaldson, editors. *Ante-Nicene Christian Library: Translations of the Writings of the Fathers Down to A.D. 325.* Vol. 1. Edinburgh, UK: T. & T. Clark, 1867.

————. *Ante-Nicene Christian Library: Translations of the Writings of the Fathers Down to A.D. 325.* Vol. 17. Edinburgh, UK: T. & T. Clark, 1870.

Tharoor, Ishaan. "7 Wicked Popes, and the Terrible Things They Did." *Washington Post,* September 24, 2015. https://www.washingtonpost.com/news/worldviews/wp/2015/09/24/7-wicked-popes-and-the-terrible-things-they-did/.

CPSIA information can be obtained
at www.ICGtesting.com
Printed in the USA
FSHW021807120919